HOW TO MAKE MONEY ONLINE

I0446596

The Ultimate Guide to Financial Freedom

JOY DANIELS

Copyright © 2023 by Joy Daniels

TABLE OF CONTENT

INTRODUCTION

Welcome to the digital frontier where opportunities for financial success abound! In my latest Amazon book, "How to Make Money Online: The Ultimate Guide to Financial Freedom," I embark on a comprehensive journey to demystify the realm of online wealth creation. As we navigate an era defined by unprecedented connectivity, this guide serves as your compass, illuminating pathways to financial independence and entrepreneurial achievement.

In a world evolving at an exponential pace, the traditional notions of work and income have undergone a transformative shift. The internet, with its vast expanse and limitless potential, has become the gateway to new and innovative avenues for generating income. This book is designed to be your indispensable companion, offering a roadmap to navigate the intricacies of the online landscape, whether you're a seasoned entrepreneur or a budding enthusiast.

I draw upon a wealth of insights gained from my experiences and extensive research, distilling them into actionable strategies that transcend the conventional norms of making money. From e-commerce ventures and affiliate marketing to freelancing and digital products, each chapter unfolds a diverse array of opportunities, equipping you with the knowledge and skills needed to thrive in the digital marketplace.

Moreover, "How to Make Money Online" goes beyond mere financial gain? It explores the concept of true financial freedom—where your income aligns with your lifestyle goals, granting you the flexibility to live life on your terms. As we delve into the intricacies of online entrepreneurship, I emphasize the importance of cultivating a mindset that embraces innovation, resilience, and adaptability.

Embark on this transformative journey with me, and let "How to Make Money Online" be your guide to unlocking the boundless possibilities that the digital world has to offer. Whether you aspire to supplement your income, escape the traditional 9-to-5 grind, or build a thriving online empire, this book is your key to realizing the potential for financial freedom in the digital age.

CHAPTER 1: THE DIGITAL LANDSCAPE UNVEILED

Welcome to the heart of the digital revolution – a realm where innovation knows no bounds and the traditional boundaries of commerce and communication have dissolved. In "The Digital Landscape Unveiled," our exploration begins at the nexus of possibility, where the online world unfolds as a vast and dynamic ecosystem of opportunities. This chapter serves as the compass, guiding you through the intricate terrain of the digital landscape, deciphering its nuances, and unveiling the manifold avenues for financial prosperity.

As we embark on this journey, we'll delve into the evolution of the digital era, dissecting the seismic shifts that have transformed the way we work, connect, and, most importantly, generate income. From the advent of the internet to the rise of social media and beyond, we'll trace the trajectory that has paved the way for the unparalleled opportunities awaiting those who navigate this landscape with insight and purpose.

"The Digital Landscape Unveiled" is not just an exploration of technology but a revelation of the profound impact it has on the entrepreneurial spirit. We'll examine the trends shaping the future of online entrepreneurship, providing you with a strategic vantage point to harness the power of the digital age.

Prepare to uncover the secrets of the virtual frontier, where the fusion of creativity, connectivity, and commerce gives rise to new possibilities. Whether you're a seasoned entrepreneur looking to expand your digital footprint or a newcomer eager to grasp the fundamentals, this chapter lays the groundwork for an exciting and transformative journey into the heart of the online realm. Let us navigate the digital landscape together, unlocking its potential and revealing the keys to financial freedom in this brave new world.

- Navigating the Online Ecosystem

Navigating the online ecosystem is a dynamic and multifaceted process that involves understanding, adapting to, and leveraging the various elements of the digital landscape. This process is essential for anyone seeking to establish a presence, build a brand, or generate income in the vast and competitive online world. Here's a breakdown of the key steps in navigating the online ecosystem:

1. **Understanding the Terrain:**

   - Explore the diverse platforms and channels available on the internet, ranging from social media and e-commerce websites to blogging platforms and online marketplaces.

   - Gain insights into the behavior of online audiences, understanding their preferences, habits, and expectations.

2. Defining Your Objectives:

- Clearly outline your goals and objectives in the online space. Whether it's building a personal brand, selling products, or providing services, having a well-defined purpose will guide your navigation.

3. Building a Strategic Presence:

- Establish a strong online presence by creating a website or blog that reflects your brand identity. Optimize it for search engines (SEO) to ensure visibility.

- Leverage social media strategically, choosing platforms that align with your target audience. Develop a consistent and compelling brand voice across all channels.

4. Engaging with Your Audience:

- Actively engage with your audience through social media, blogs, forums, and other online communities. Foster meaningful connections by responding to comments, addressing inquiries, and participating in relevant conversations.

5. Monitoring and Analyzing Performance:

- Utilize analytics tools to monitor the performance of your online efforts. Track website traffic, social media engagement, and other relevant metrics to assess what is working and where adjustments are needed.

6. Adapting to Trends and Changes:

- Stay informed about industry trends, algorithm changes, and emerging technologies. The online landscape is dynamic, and adapting to shifts in trends and consumer behavior is crucial for sustained success.

7. Networking and Collaboration:

- Build relationships with influencers, peers, and other entities in your niche. Networking can open doors to collaborations, partnerships, and opportunities for growth.

8. Ensuring Security and Compliance:

- Prioritize online security to protect your digital assets and sensitive information. Familiarize yourself with data protection regulations and ensure compliance to maintain trust with your audience.

Navigating the online ecosystem is an ongoing process that requires continuous learning, adaptability, and a strategic mindset. By understanding the landscape, setting clear goals, and actively engaging with your audience, you can navigate the complexities of the digital world and position yourself for success in the online marketplace.

- Evolution of Work and Income in the Digital Era

The evolution of work and income in the digital era has been a transformative journey, reshaping traditional employment structures and giving rise to new opportunities for individuals and businesses alike. Several key factors have contributed to this evolution:

1. **Remote Work and Digital Nomadism:**

   - The advent of the internet has facilitated the rise of remote work, allowing individuals to perform tasks and jobs from virtually anywhere in the world.

   - Digital nomadism has emerged as a lifestyle choice for those who leverage technology to work remotely while embracing a location-independent lifestyle.

2. **Gig Economy and Freelancing:**

   - Online platforms have democratized access to work, giving rise to the gig economy. Freelancers can now offer their skills and services on platforms like Upwork, Fiverr, and others, connecting with clients globally.

   - This shift has empowered individuals to pursue flexible work arrangements, choose their projects, and diversify their income streams.

3. **E-Commerce and Entrepreneurship:**

   - The rise of e-commerce platforms such as Amazon, Etsy, and Shopify has enabled individuals to become online entrepreneurs. Digital storefronts empower people to sell products and reach a global customer base.

- Dropshipping, print-on-demand, and affiliate marketing are examples of business models that leverage the digital landscape for income generation.

4. **Automation and Artificial Intelligence:**

- Automation and AI technologies have transformed industries, automating routine tasks and creating new job categories.

- While some jobs have been displaced, the digital era has also seen the emergence of roles focused on developing, managing, and maintaining these technologies.

5. **Monetization of Content:**

- Content creators, whether in the form of bloggers, vloggers, podcasters, or social media influencers, have found new avenues to monetize their content.

- Ad revenue, sponsorships, affiliate marketing, and crowdfunding are strategies employed by content creators to generate income directly from their audiences.

6. Cryptocurrencies and Decentralized Finance (DeFi):

- The rise of cryptocurrencies and blockchain technology has introduced new possibilities for decentralized finance. Cryptocurrencies provide alternative avenues for investment, trading, and income generation.

- DeFi platforms offer decentralized lending, staking, and liquidity provision, allowing individuals to participate in financial activities outside of traditional banking systems.

7. Rise of Online Education and Skill Monetization:

- Online learning platforms have democratized education, enabling individuals to acquire new skills and knowledge remotely.

- Entrepreneurs can monetize their expertise by creating and selling online courses, webinars, and digital products.

8. **Collaborative and Shared Economy:**

- Platforms like Airbnb, Uber, and TaskRabbit exemplify the collaborative economy, where individuals can share resources, services, and skills for mutual benefit.

- This model has expanded to various industries, fostering economic participation and resource optimization.

The evolution of work and income in the digital era reflects a paradigm shift towards flexibility, decentralization, and accessibility. While presenting new opportunities, it also necessitates adaptability and continuous skill development to thrive in an ever-changing landscape. Individuals who embrace digital transformation can unlock diverse pathways to financial success and career fulfilment.

- Trends Shaping the Future of Online Entrepreneurship

The future of online entrepreneurship is shaped by dynamic trends that respond to evolving consumer behaviors, technological advancements, and global economic shifts. Entrepreneurs who anticipate and adapt to these trends position themselves for success in the competitive digital landscape. Here are key trends shaping the future of online entrepreneurship:

1. **E-Commerce Innovation:**

   - Continuous innovation in e-commerce, including augmented reality (AR) shopping experiences, virtual try-ons, and personalized recommendations, enhances the online shopping journey.

   - Direct-to-consumer (DTC) models and subscription-based services are gaining popularity, fostering brand loyalty and customer retention.

2. Rise of Sustainable and Ethical Entrepreneurship:

- Consumers are increasingly conscious of sustainability and ethical business practices. Entrepreneurs are incorporating eco-friendly practices, ethical sourcing, and social responsibility into their business models to align with consumer values.

3. Remote Work and Digital Collaboration:

- The trend towards remote work has accelerated, leading to a surge in digital collaboration tools and platforms. Entrepreneurs are leveraging virtual teams, fostering global talent collaboration, and redefining traditional office structures.

4. NFTs and Blockchain Technology:

- Non-fungible tokens (NFTs) and blockchain technology are transforming how digital assets, art, and collectables are owned, sold, and traded.

Entrepreneurs are exploring new business models and opportunities within the blockchain space.

5. Innovations in Artificial Intelligence (AI) and Automation:

- AI and automation are revolutionizing business processes, customer service, and data analysis. Entrepreneurs are adopting AI to enhance productivity, streamline operations, and personalize user experiences.

6. Digital Health and Wellness:

- The integration of technology into health and wellness entrepreneurship is on the rise. Online fitness classes, health apps, and personalized wellness solutions cater to a growing demand for digital health services.

7. Content Monetization and Membership Models:

- Content creators are diversifying revenue streams through subscription models, exclusive memberships, and premium content. Platforms like

Patreon and Substack enable entrepreneurs to monetize their creative endeavours directly from their audience.

8. Virtual and Augmented Reality Experiences:

- Virtual and augmented reality technologies are transforming industries such as gaming, education, and real estate. Entrepreneurs are exploring immersive experiences and virtual storefronts to engage customers in novel ways.

9. Social Commerce and Influencer Marketing:

- Social media platforms continue to evolve as powerful e-commerce channels. Entrepreneurs leverage social commerce features, collaborate with influencers, and utilize user-generated content to drive brand awareness and sales.

10. Decentralized Finance (DeFi) and Cryptocurrency:

- Entrepreneurs are exploring opportunities in decentralized finance (DeFi) and the cryptocurrency space. This includes blockchain-based financial services, decentralized exchanges, and innovative applications within the decentralized finance ecosystem.

11. **Personalization and Data Privacy:**

- Entrepreneurs are focusing on hyper-personalization by leveraging customer data responsibly. Striking a balance between personalization and respecting data privacy regulations is crucial for building and maintaining customer trust.

12. **Cybersecurity and Trust Building:**

- With the increasing prevalence of online transactions, cybersecurity becomes paramount. Entrepreneurs prioritize robust cybersecurity measures to protect customer data and build trust in their digital platforms.

By staying attuned to these trends, online entrepreneurs can position themselves as innovators, stay ahead of the curve, and capitalize on emerging opportunities in the ever-evolving digital landscape. Adaptability, a commitment to customer-centric approaches, and a willingness to embrace new technologies will be key factors in navigating the future of online entrepreneurship.

CHAPTER 2: BUILDING YOUR ONLINE FOUNDATION

Welcome to the pivotal chapter, "Building Your Online Foundation," where the journey to digital success begins with the establishment of a robust and strategic groundwork. In the ever-expanding realm of online entrepreneurship, creating a solid foundation is akin to laying the cornerstone of a skyscraper – a critical step that determines the structure's stability, resilience, and potential for growth.

This chapter serves as your blueprint for crafting an online presence that not only reflects your vision and values but also resonates powerfully with your target audience. Whether you're an aspiring entrepreneur looking to make your mark or a seasoned professional seeking to amplify your digital footprint, the principles outlined here will guide you through the essential steps of building a compelling online foundation.

We will explore the intricate art of defining your passion and niche, understanding the significance of a distinctive personal brand, and establishing an online presence that goes beyond a mere website. The journey begins with introspection, extends into the realm of strategic brand development, and culminates in the creation of a digital home that not only showcases your offerings but also engages and captivates your audience.

As we delve into the core elements of building your online foundation, keep in mind that this is more than a technical endeavor – it's an opportunity to articulate your story, values, and unique selling propositions in a way that resonates with the digital world. By the end of this chapter, you'll not only have a digital home but a strategically crafted foundation that propels you forward in the competitive landscape of online entrepreneurship. So, let's embark on this transformative journey of building a digital foundation that stands the test of time and serves as the launch pad for your online success.

- Identifying Your Passion and Niche

Identifying your passion and niche is a pivotal step in building a strong foundation for your online presence. This process involves self-reflection, market analysis, and strategic decision-making to align your interests with market demand. Here's a detailed exploration of the steps involved in identifying your passion and niche:

1. **Self-Reflection:**

 - *Explore Your Interests:* Begin by reflecting on your interests, hobbies, and skills. Identify areas that genuinely excite and inspire you.

 - *Assess Your Strengths:* Consider your strengths and expertise. What skills do you possess that set you apart? What are you passionate about sharing with others?

2. Market Research:

- *Identify Market Trends:* Research current market trends and assess consumer needs. Look for gaps or underserved areas where your passion aligns with potential demand.

- *Competitor Analysis:* Study competitors in your field of interest. Identify their strengths, weaknesses, and unique selling propositions to find your niche.

3. Define Your Unique Value Proposition (UVP):

- *Clarify Your Offering:* Clearly define what you can offer to your audience. What makes your approach unique? How can you solve a problem or meet a need that others may not be addressing?

- *Align with Your Passion:* Ensure that your unique value proposition resonates with your passion. The intersection of your interests and market demand is where your niche lies.

4. Consider Target Audience:

- ***Identify Your Audience:*** Determine the demographics and characteristics of your target audience. Who are the people most likely to connect with your passion and benefit from your offerings?

- ***Understand Their Needs:*** Understand the needs, challenges, and aspirations of your target audience. Tailor your niche to address these specific concerns.

5. Test and Iterate:

- ***Start Small:*** Begin with a small-scale test of your niche. This could be through a blog, social media, or a minimal viable product (MVP).

- ***Gather Feedback:*** Pay attention to audience feedback. What resonates with them? What aspects of your passion are most appealing? Use this information to refine your niche.

6. Evaluate Long-Term Viability:

- ***Assess Sustainability:*** Consider the long-term sustainability of your chosen niche. Is there growth potential, or is it a passing trend?

- *Adaptability:* Choose a niche that allows for adaptability. The digital landscape evolves, and your ability to pivot or expand within your passion is crucial.

7. **Align with Your Values:**

- *Integrate Personal Values:* Ensure that your chosen niche aligns with your values. Authenticity is key to building a genuine connection with your audience.

- *Passion-Driven Content:* Craft content and offerings that stem from your genuine enthusiasm. This authenticity will resonate with your audience.

Identifying your passion and niche is an ongoing process that may evolve. It's a delicate balance between personal fulfilment and meeting the needs of your target audience. By carefully navigating this process, you set the stage for a strong and authentic online presence that reflects your passion while establishing a meaningful connection with your audience.

- Creating a Solid Personal Brand

Creating a solid personal brand is a fundamental aspect of building a strong online foundation. Your brand is how you present yourself to the world, conveying your identity, values, and unique attributes. Here's a comprehensive guide to the process of creating a solid personal brand:

1. **Self-Discovery:**

 - *Define Your Values:* Identify your core values and principles. What do you stand for? What matters most to you personally and professionally?

 - *Identify Strengths and Weaknesses:* Assess your strengths, skills, and weaknesses. Understanding what sets you apart is crucial for crafting a distinctive personal brand.

2. Define Your Unique Selling Proposition (USP):

- *Identify Your Niche:* Connect your brand with your niche. What makes you unique in your field or industry? Define your unique selling proposition that sets you apart from others.

3. Craft a Consistent Message:

- *Define Your Message:* Develop a clear and concise message that communicates your values, expertise, and mission. This message should resonate across all platforms and interactions.

- *Consistency is Key:* Maintain consistency in your messaging, visuals, and tone across social media, your website, and any other channels where you have a presence.

4. Build an Online Presence:

- *Create a Professional Website:* Establish a personal website as the central hub for your brand. This is where you can showcase your portfolio, and achievements, and provide a glimpse into your personality.

  - *Optimize Social Media Profiles:* Curate professional and engaging social media profiles. Use platforms like LinkedIn, Twitter, and Instagram strategically to reinforce your brand.

5. Develop a Visual Identity:

  - *Design a Logo and Visual Elements:* Create a professional logo and visual elements that represent your brand. Consistent visuals contribute to brand recognition.

  - *Use High-Quality Imagery:* Invest in high-quality images and graphics that align with your brand's aesthetics.

6. Content Strategy:

  - *Content Alignment:* Develop a content strategy that aligns with your brand message. Create valuable, shareable content that reinforces your expertise and adds value to your audience.

- Share Personal Stories: Humanize your brand by sharing personal stories and experiences. This fosters a genuine connection with your audience.

7. Engage Authentically:

- Authentic Interaction: Engage authentically with your audience. Respond to comments, participate in conversations, and showcase your personality.

- Networking: Build meaningful connections within your industry. Networking both online and offline contributes to the growth of your brand.

8. Seek Endorsements and Testimonials:

- Request Recommendations: On platforms like LinkedIn, actively seek recommendations and endorsements from colleagues, clients, or collaborators. Positive testimonials add credibility to your brand.

9. Continuous Evaluation and Adaptation:

- Monitor Your Brand's Perception: Regularly assess how your brand is perceived. Pay attention to

feedback, analytics, and audience interactions to adapt and refine your brand strategy.

  - *Adapt to Growth and Changes:* As your career evolves, be prepared to adapt your brand. Embrace growth, new experiences, and shifts in your professional focus.

10. **Invest in Professional Development:**

  - *Continuous Learning:* Stay updated on industry trends, acquire new skills, and demonstrate a commitment to continuous learning. This reinforces your expertise and adds value to your brand.

Creating a solid personal brand is an ongoing process that evolves with your personal and professional growth. By staying authentic, consistent, and focused on delivering value, you can cultivate a powerful personal brand that resonates with your target audience and distinguishes you in the digital landscape.

- Establishing an Online Presence: Websites and Social Media

Establishing a strong online presence through websites and social media is essential for individuals and businesses aiming to connect with a global audience, showcase their offerings, and build brand authority. Here's a comprehensive guide to the process of establishing an online presence:

1. **Define Your Goals:**

- *Identify Objectives:* Clarify your goals for establishing an online presence. Whether it's brand awareness, lead generation, or sales, having clear objectives guides your strategy.

2. **Create a Professional Website:**

- *Choose a Domain Name:* Select a memorable and relevant domain name for your website. Ensure it reflects your brand and is easy to remember.

- ***Select a Web Hosting Provider:*** Choose a reliable web hosting provider that aligns with your website's needs in terms of speed, security, and scalability.

- ***Design Your Website:*** Create a visually appealing and user-friendly website. Use consistent branding elements, high-quality visuals, and an intuitive layout.

- ***Optimize for Search Engines (SEO):*** Implement SEO best practices to enhance your website's visibility in search engine results.

3. Leverage Social Media Platforms:

- ***Choose Relevant Platforms:*** Identify the social media platforms that align with your brand and target audience. Examples include LinkedIn for professionals, Instagram for visual content, and Twitter for real-time updates.

- ***Optimize Profiles:*** Craft compelling and complete social media profiles. Use consistent branding elements, including profile pictures, cover photos and bio information.

- Develop a Content Strategy: Plan a content strategy that resonates with your audience. Include a mix of informative, engaging, and promotional content.

- Utilize Visual Content: Visuals are crucial in social media. Incorporate high-quality images, graphics, and videos to enhance engagement.

- Engage with Your Audience: Actively engage with your audience by responding to comments, participating in discussions, and fostering a sense of community.

4. **Integrate Cross-Platform Branding:**

- Consistent Branding: Maintain consistency in branding across your website and social media platforms. Use similar colors, fonts, and messaging to reinforce your brand identity.

- Linking Between Platforms: Provide links on your website to your social media profiles, and vice versa. Cross-linking helps users discover and connect with you across platforms.

5. Implement Blogging and Content Marketing:

- *Start a Blog:* If relevant to your brand, start a blog on your website. Regularly publish high-quality, valuable content that establishes you as an authority in your field.

- *Promote Content on Social Media:* Share blog posts and other content across your social media platforms to drive traffic to your website.

6. Collect and Showcase Testimonials:

- *Encourage Reviews and Testimonials:* Actively seek reviews and testimonials from satisfied customers or clients. Display them prominently on your website and share them on social media to build trust.

7. Monitor Analytics and Adjust Strategy:

- *Use Analytics Tools:* Employ website analytics tools (e.g., Google Analytics) and social media insights to track performance. Monitor metrics such as website traffic, engagement, and conversion rates.

- *Iterate Based on Data:* Analyze the data regularly and adjust your strategy accordingly. Identify what works well and optimize areas that need improvement.

8. Stay Updated on Trends:

- *Keep Abreast of Industry Trends:* Stay informed about evolving trends in website design, social media algorithms, and digital marketing. Adapt your strategy to incorporate emerging practices.

9. Invest in Security Measures:

- *Secure Your Website:* Implement security measures to protect your website from potential threats. Use SSL certificates for secure data transmission and regularly update software.

10. Encourage User Interaction:

- *Incorporate Interactive Elements:* Foster user interaction on your website, such as comment sections, forums, or interactive features. On social media, run polls, quizzes, and contests to engage your audience.

11. **Mobile Optimization:**

- *Optimize for Mobile Devices:* Ensure that your website and social media content are optimized for mobile users. A responsive design is crucial for a seamless user experience.

Establishing an online presence is an ongoing process that requires dedication, adaptability, and a commitment to delivering value to your audience. By combining an effective website with a strategic social media presence, you can create a comprehensive and compelling online presence that elevates your brand and fosters meaningful connections with your audience.

CHAPTER 3: DIVERSE AVENUES FOR ONLINE INCOME

Welcome to the expansive realm of "Diverse Avenues for Online Income," a chapter that unravels the tapestry of opportunities available in the digital landscape. In an era marked by unprecedented connectivity and technological innovation, how individuals can generate income online is as diverse as the passions and skills that drive them. This chapter serves as your guide to exploring and navigating the myriad paths leading to financial success in the vast online marketplace.

Whether you're a budding entrepreneur seeking to monetize your creativity, a freelancer aiming to leverage your skills, or an e-commerce enthusiast eager to build a thriving online business, the possibilities are both exciting and limitless. We delve into a spectrum of online income streams, ranging from established models to cutting-edge trends, providing insights, strategies, and practical advice for individuals at every stage of their online income journey.

From e-commerce ventures and affiliate marketing to freelancing, digital products, and content creation, each avenue unfolds with its unique set of opportunities and challenges. The digital age has democratized access to income-generating activities, allowing individuals to carve out their niches and pursue financial success in alignment with their passions.

As we embark on this exploration of diverse online income avenues, keep in mind that the landscape is dynamic and ever-evolving. The strategies outlined in this chapter are designed to empower you with the knowledge and tools needed to thrive in the digital marketplace, adapt to emerging trends, and cultivate a sustainable and fulfilling online income.

Get ready to unlock the doors to financial opportunity and innovation as we navigate through the diverse avenues for online income. Whether you're seeking additional streams of revenue, planning to escape the traditional 9-to-5 grind, or aspiring to build a digital empire, this chapter is your compass to navigate the exciting and boundless world of online income possibilities.

- E-Commerce: Launching and Scaling Your Online Store

E-commerce has emerged as a dynamic and lucrative avenue for entrepreneurs, offering a platform to showcase products, connect with a global audience, and build thriving online businesses. Whether you're a budding entrepreneur or an established retailer looking to expand your digital footprint, the process of launching and scaling your online store involves strategic planning, technological proficiency, and a keen understanding of consumer behavior.

Launching Your Online Store:

1. Market Research and Niche Identification:

- *Understand Your Audience:* Conduct thorough market research to identify your target audience, their preferences, and purchasing behaviors.

- *Choose a Niche:* Select a niche that aligns with your expertise and market demand. A focused approach can set your store apart.

2. Selecting the Right E-Commerce Platform:

- *Evaluate Platforms:* Choose a reliable e-commerce platform such as Shopify, WooCommerce, or Magento based on your business needs, scalability, and technical proficiency.

- *Customization and User Experience:* Opt for a platform that allows customization to create a seamless and user-friendly online shopping experience.

3. Product Listings and Descriptions:

- *High-Quality Imagery:* Showcase your products with high-quality images that provide a clear view from multiple angles.

- *Compelling Descriptions:* Craft compelling product descriptions that highlight features, benefits, and unique selling points.

4. Secure Payment Gateways:

- *Prioritize Security:* Integrate secure payment gateways to build trust with customers. Options like PayPal, Stripe, and others ensure secure transactions.

5. Mobile Optimization:

- *Responsive Design:* Optimize your online store for mobile devices. A responsive design ensures a seamless shopping experience across various screen sizes.

6. **Implementing SEO Strategies:**

 - *Keyword Optimization:* Incorporate relevant keywords in product titles, descriptions, and Meta tags to improve search engine visibility.

 - *Create Quality Content:* Develop blog content and product descriptions that not only engage customers but also enhance SEO.

 Scaling Your Online Store:

1. **Data-Driven Decision Making:**

 - *Analytics Integration:* Implement analytics tools to track customer behavior, sales patterns, and website traffic.

 - *Iterative Improvements:* Use data insights to make informed decisions for optimizing your product offerings, marketing strategies, and user experience.

2. Expanding Product Lines and Categories:

- *Diversification:* Introduce new products or expand into related categories to appeal to a broader audience.

- *Monitor Trends*: Stay attuned to market trends and consumer preferences to adapt and innovate your product offerings.

3. Customer Engagement and Retention:

- *Email Marketing:* Build and leverage an email subscriber list for targeted marketing campaigns and promotions.

- *Loyalty Programs:* Implement loyalty programs to reward repeat customers and encourage brand loyalty.

4. Social Media Integration:

- *Strategic Social Media Marketing:* Utilize social media platforms to showcase products, run promotions, and engage with your audience.

- *User-Generated Content*: Encourage customers to share their experiences and feature user-generated content to enhance brand authenticity.

5. Optimizing Checkout Process:

- *Streamlined Checkout:* Simplify the checkout process to minimize cart abandonment. Implement guest checkout options and offer multiple payment methods.

6. Scalable Infrastructure:

- *Cloud Hosting:* Consider scalable cloud hosting solutions to accommodate increased website traffic during peak times.

- *Inventory Management Systems:* Implement robust inventory management systems to handle growing product lines efficiently.

7. Customer Feedback and Reviews:

- *Feedback Collection:* Encourage customers to provide feedback and reviews. Address concerns promptly and use positive reviews as testimonials on your website.

8. Strategic Partnerships:

- *Collaborations:* Explore collaborations with influencers, other brands, or complementary businesses to expand your reach.

- *Affiliate Marketing:* Implement affiliate marketing programs to leverage partnerships for mutual benefit.

Launching and scaling your online store is a journey that requires continuous adaptation, innovation, and a commitment to delivering exceptional customer experiences. By integrating technological advancements, data-driven insights, and customer-centric strategies, you can position your e-commerce venture for sustained growth and success in the competitive digital marketplace.

- Mastering Affiliate Marketing Strategies

Affiliate marketing is a performance-based marketing strategy where businesses reward affiliates (partners) for driving traffic or sales to the business's products or services. To succeed in affiliate marketing, both merchants and affiliates need to implement effective strategies. Here's a comprehensive discussion of affiliate marketing strategies:

For Merchants:

1. **Clear Program Structure:**

- Establish a transparent commission structure, providing affiliates with a clear understanding of how they'll be compensated for their efforts.

2. **Attractive Commission Rates:**

- Offer competitive commission rates to attract and retain high-performing affiliates. Consider tiered structures based on performance levels.

3. **Quality Affiliate Recruitment:**

- Select affiliates strategically, focusing on those who align with your brand values and have an audience that matches your target market.

4. Comprehensive Affiliate Resources:

- Provide affiliates with marketing materials, product information, and creatives that make it easy for them to promote your products effectively.

5. Regular Communication:

- Establish open lines of communication with affiliates. Regularly update them on promotions, new products, and any changes to the affiliate program.

6. Incentives and Bonuses:

- Offer bonuses or special incentives for affiliates who consistently perform well or achieve specific targets. This encourages ongoing engagement and enthusiasm.

7. Cookie Duration and Attribution Models:

- Choose an appropriate cookie duration that strikes a balance between rewarding affiliates for their efforts and respecting customer decision-making time.

- Implement clear attribution models to ensure fair credit allocation for conversions.

8. Conversion Tracking:

- Use reliable tracking tools and technologies to accurately measure affiliate-driven conversions. This data is crucial for optimizing your program.

For Affiliates:

1. Choose Relevant Products:

- Select products or services that resonate with your audience and align with your content. Authenticity builds trust and enhances conversion rates.

2. Quality Content Creation:

- Create high-quality content that educates, entertains, or solves problems. Whether its blog posts, videos, or social media content, relevance is key.

3. Deep Linking:

- Implement deep linking to direct visitors to specific product pages rather than just the homepage. This enhances the user experience and increases the likelihood of conversions.

4. Multichannel Promotion:

- Diversify your promotional channels. Combine content marketing, social media promotion, email marketing, and other channels to reach a broader audience.

5. Building Email Lists:

- Encourage your audience to subscribe to your email list. Email marketing allows you to nurture leads and promote affiliate products effectively.

6. Engage with Your Audience:

- Build a relationship with your audience. Respond to comments, engage in discussions, and create a community around your content.

7. Stay Informed and Adaptive:

- Stay updated on industry trends, product updates, and changes to the affiliate program. Being informed enables you to adapt your strategies effectively.

8. A/B Testing:

- Experiment with different strategies, creatives, and promotional methods. A/B testing helps you identify what resonates best with your audience.

9. Compliance with Regulations:

- Familiarize yourself with legal and ethical guidelines regarding affiliate marketing. Be transparent with your audience about affiliate relationships.

10. Performance Analysis:

- Regularly analyze your performance metrics. Understand which strategies are driving results and optimize your approach accordingly.

For Both Merchants and Affiliates:

1. **Transparency and Trust:**

   - Foster transparency and trust between merchants and affiliates. Clear communication and honesty contribute to long-term, mutually beneficial relationships.

2. Continuous Optimization:

   - Regularly assess and optimize your strategies based on performance data. This includes tweaking commission structures, refining content, and adjusting promotional tactics.

3. **Adaptability:**

   - Be adaptable to changes in the industry, consumer behavior, and technological advancements. What works today may need adjustment tomorrow.

4. **Compliance with Policies:**

   - Adhere to the terms and conditions of the affiliate program. Merchants should ensure their program is compliant with legal and industry standards.

Successful affiliate marketing is a collaborative effort that requires a strategic approach, mutual understanding, and ongoing refinement of tactics. By implementing these strategies, both merchants and affiliates can maximize the benefits of affiliate marketing and create a win-win scenario for all parties involved.

- Freelancing: Tapping into Your Skills for Profit

Freelancing has become a cornerstone of the modern workforce, offering individuals the opportunity to leverage their skills and talents independently for profit. Whether you're a writer, designer, programmer, marketer, or possess any specialized skill, freelancing provides a flexible and dynamic avenue to turn your expertise into a lucrative venture. Here's a comprehensive discussion on freelancing, tapping into your skills for profit:

1. **Identifying Your Niche and Skillset:**

- *Self-Assessment:* Begin by conducting an honest assessment of your skills, strengths, and areas of expertise.

- *Niche Selection:* Identify a specific niche or industry where your skills are in demand. Specialization can set you apart in a competitive market.

2. **Building an Impressive Portfolio:**

- *Showcasing Work:* Create a portfolio that highlights your best work and demonstrates the range and quality of your skills.

- *Client Testimonials:* Request testimonials from previous clients to add credibility to your portfolio.

3. Establishing Your Online Presence:

- *Professional Website:* Create a professional website that serves as a central hub for showcasing your portfolio, skills, and contact information.

- *LinkedIn Profile:* Optimize your LinkedIn profile with a professional photo, comprehensive work history, and endorsements from colleagues.

4. Choosing Freelance Platforms:

- *Upwork, Fiverr, Freelancer:* Join popular freelance platforms to access a vast pool of clients. Craft a compelling profile, clearly stating your skills, rates, and availability.

- *Niche-Specific Platforms*: Explore industry-specific platforms tailored to your skills, such as GitHub for developers or Behance for designers.

5. Setting Competitive Rates:

- *Market Research:* Research industry standards and competitor rates to set a competitive pricing structure.

- *Value-Based Pricing:* Consider the value you bring to clients and price accordingly. Communicate the benefits of your services in your proposals.

6. Effective Proposal Writing:

- *Personalized Proposals:* Tailor your proposals to each client, demonstrating a clear understanding of their needs and how your skills can address them.

- Highlighting Experience: Emphasize relevant experience and showcase how your skills have solved similar challenges in the past.

7. Time Management and Productivity:

- *Set Clear Goals:* Establish daily or weekly goals to stay on track and manage your workload effectively.

- *Use Productivity Tools:* Employ tools like Trello, Asana, or time-tracking apps to enhance organization and efficiency.

8. Communication and Client Management:

- *Clear Communication:* Foster transparent and effective communication with clients. Set expectations early on regarding deliverables, timelines, and communication channels.

- *Client Relationship Building:* Cultivate positive relationships with clients to encourage repeat business and referrals.

9. Continuous Learning and Skill Enhancement:

- **Stay Updated:** Keep abreast of industry trends and advancements. Continuous learning enhances your skillset and keeps you competitive.

- *Professional Development:* Invest in courses, workshops, or certifications to deepen your expertise and diversify your skill portfolio.

10. Financial Management:

- *Invoicing and Payments:* Establish a clear invoicing system and specify payment terms. Utilize platforms with secure payment gateways.

- *Savings and Taxes:* Set aside a portion of your earnings for taxes and create a savings plan for variable income months.

11. Networking and Building a Reputation:

- *Attend Industry Events:* Participate in conferences, webinars, and networking events to connect with potential clients and other freelancers.

- *Social Media Engagement:* Actively engage on social media platforms within your industry. Share insights, participate in discussions, and showcase your work.

12. Handling Challenges and Rejections:

- *Resilience:* Freelancing comes with challenges, including rejection and difficult clients. Develop resilience and view challenges as opportunities for growth.

- *Feedback Incorporation:* Learn from rejections and client feedback. Use constructive criticism to refine your skills and approach.

Freelancing is a journey that combines your passion with the pursuit of financial independence. By tapping into your skills, building a strong online presence, and adopting effective business strategies, you can turn freelancing into a sustainable and fulfilling career. The key lies in continuous improvement, adaptability, and a commitment to delivering value to your clients.

- Creating and Selling Digital Products

Creating and selling digital products is an excellent way to monetize your skills, knowledge, and creativity in the online marketplace. Whether you're an artist, writer, programmer, or expert in a specific field, digital products offer a scalable and passive income stream. Here's a comprehensive discussion of the process of creating and selling digital products:

1. **Identify Your Niche and Audience:**

- *Niche Selection:* Define a specific niche or target audience based on your expertise and the demand in the market.

- *Audience Research:* Understand the needs, preferences, and challenges of your target audience to create products that address their specific concerns.

2. **Choose the Type of Digital Product:**

- *Ebooks and Guides:* Share your knowledge through comprehensive guides or ebooks.

- *Online Courses:* Create structured courses using platforms like Udemy, Teachable, or your website.

- *Digital Art and Design:* Sell digital art, illustrations, or design assets on platforms like Etsy or Gumroad.

- *Software and Tools:* Develop and sell digital tools, templates, or software that solve a particular problem.

3. Create High-Quality Content:

- ***Thorough Research:*** Invest time in researching and ensuring the accuracy of the information you provide.

- ***Engaging Design:*** For visual products, focus on creating eye-catching designs and layouts.

- Clarity and Structure: Ensure that your content is well-organized, easy to understand, and adds value to your audience.

4. Choose the Right Tools and Platforms:

- ***E-commerce Platforms:*** Utilize platforms like Shopify, Gumroad, or Etsy for selling digital products.

- ***Learning Management Systems (LMS):*** If creating courses, explore LMS platforms like Teachable, Thinkific, or Moodle.

- ***Digital Delivery Systems:*** Use systems that automate the delivery of digital products to customers after purchase.

5. **Optimize for Search Engines (SEO):**

- *Keyword Optimization:* Optimize product titles, descriptions, and tags for relevant keywords to improve visibility on search engines and platforms.

- *Create a Landing Page:* If applicable, create a dedicated landing page for your digital product to enhance its online presence.

6. **Set Competitive Pricing:**

- *Market Research:* Research the pricing of similar digital products in your niche.

- *Value-Based Pricing:* Consider the value your product provides to users when setting prices.

7. **Build a Sales Funnel:**

- *Lead Generation:* Offer free content or resources related to your digital product to build an email list and generate leads.

- **Email Marketing:** Utilize email campaigns to nurture leads and guide them towards purchasing your digital product.

8. Create Compelling Sales Copy:

 - *Benefits-Oriented Copy:* Highlight the benefits and outcomes users can expect from your digital product.

 - *Clear Call-to-Action (CTA):* Include a clear and persuasive call-to-action to prompt users to make a purchase.

9. Implement Secure Payment Options:

 - *Payment Gateways:* Integrate secure payment gateways like PayPal, Stripe, or other trusted options.

 - *SSL Certificate:* Ensure your website has an SSL certificate to encrypt transactions and build trust with customers.

10. Offer Customer Support:

 - *Clear Communication:* Provide clear instructions for accessing and using your digital product.

- *Prompt Response:* Be responsive to customer inquiries and troubleshoot any issues promptly.

11. Market Your Digital Product:

- *Social Media Marketing:* Leverage social media platforms to promote your digital product. Create engaging content, share testimonials, and run targeted ads.

- *Affiliate Marketing:* Partner with affiliates to expand your product's reach and increase sales.

- *Content Marketing:* Share valuable content related to your product to attract and engage your target audience.

12. Collect and Analyze Data:

- *Analytics Tools:* Utilize analytics tools to track sales, customer behavior, and other relevant metrics.

- *Iterative Improvements:* Use data insights to make informed decisions and continually improve your digital product and marketing strategies.

13. Legal Considerations:

- **Terms of Service and Licensing:** Clearly outline the terms of service, licensing agreements, and usage rights for your digital product.

- **Digital Rights Management (DRM):** Depending on the nature of your product, consider implementing DRM to protect against unauthorized distribution.

14. Customer Feedback and Iteration:

- **Feedback Collection:** Encourage customers to provide feedback and reviews.

- **Iterative Improvement:** Use feedback to make necessary improvements and updates to your digital product.

Creating and selling digital products is a dynamic and evolving process. By consistently refining your approach, staying attuned to market trends, and actively engaging with your audience, you can establish a successful digital product business that provides both value to your customers and a sustainable income stream for yourself.

CHAPTER 4: THE ART OF MONETIZING CONTENT

Welcome to "The Art of Monetizing Content," a chapter that delves into the strategic and creative ways of turning your passion and expertise into a sustainable income stream. In the digital age, where content reigns supreme, individuals and businesses alike have the unprecedented opportunity to capitalize on their creations, insights, and skills. Whether you're a writer, artist, podcaster, or any content creator, this chapter serves as a guide to unlocking the pathways to financial success while navigating the intricate art of content monetization.

In a landscape characterized by diverse platforms, evolving audience behaviors, and innovative business models, the ability to monetize content is both an art and a science. From understanding your audience and choosing the right monetization methods to building a loyal following and optimizing revenue streams, we explore the multifaceted facets that make up the canvas of content monetization.

Through this chapter, we embark on a journey to explore various content monetization strategies, including advertising, subscriptions, affiliate marketing, and digital products. We'll delve into the nuances of each method, providing insights, practical tips, and real-world examples to empower you to make informed decisions that align with your goals and resonate with your audience.

Whether you're a seasoned content creator looking to diversify your revenue streams or a newcomer eager to turn your passion into profit, "The Art of Monetizing Content" is designed to be your companion in the exciting and dynamic realm of content entrepreneurship. As we navigate through the intricacies of this art, remember that success lies not just in the mastery of techniques but also in the authenticity and value you bring to your audience.

Get ready to unleash the full potential of your content and embark on a journey where creativity meets commerce, passion transforms into profit, and the art of content monetization becomes a skill you can master to create a sustainable and rewarding digital presence.

- Blogging for Profit: Strategies and Pitfalls

"Blogging for Profit: Strategies and Pitfalls" is a nuanced exploration into the world of content creation where individuals seek not only to share their passions and insights but also to turn their blogs into profitable ventures. This discussion encompasses both the strategic approaches that can lead to financial success and the potential pitfalls that bloggers may encounter on their journey.

Strategies for Profitable Blogging:

1. Identify Your Niche:

- *Focused Content:* Define a specific niche that aligns with your expertise and audience's interests. Specialization enhances your authority and attracts a dedicated readership.

2. Create High-Quality Content:

- *Value and Relevance:* Develop content that provides genuine value to your audience. In-depth, well-researched articles are more likely to attract and retain readers.

- *Consistency:* Maintain a regular posting schedule to keep your audience engaged and returning for more.

3. Leverage SEO:

- *Keyword Optimization:* Incorporate relevant keywords in your content to improve search engine visibility.

- *Meta Tags and Descriptions:* Optimize meta tags and descriptions to enhance click-through rates from search engine results.

4. Build a Loyal Audience:

- *Engagement:* Foster engagement through comments, social media, and newsletters. A loyal audience is more likely to support your monetization efforts.

- *Email Marketing:* Develop an email list to communicate directly with your audience, share updates, and promote products or services.

5. Monetization Methods:

- *Advertising:* Implement display ads or native ads to generate revenue. Google AdSense and affiliate marketing are common approaches.

- *Affiliate Marketing:* Promote products or services and earn a commission for every sale or lead generated through your unique affiliate link.

- *Sponsored Content:* Collaborate with brands for sponsored posts or partnerships.

6. **Offer Digital Products:**

- *Ebooks, Courses, or Webinars:* Create and sell digital products that align with your blog's niche. This could include educational resources, guides, or exclusive content.

- *Printables or Merchandise:* Explore the sale of branded merchandise or downloadable printable.

7. **Membership and Subscription Models:**

- *Exclusive Content:* Provide premium content or services to subscribers who pay a recurring fee.

- *Online Communities:* Establish a private community or forum accessible to paying members.

8. **Diversify Income Streams:**

- *Multiple Platforms:* Explore revenue streams beyond your blog, such as YouTube, podcasts, or social media platforms.

- *Freelance Opportunities:* Leverage your blog as a portfolio to secure freelance writing or consulting gigs.

Pitfalls to Watch Out For:

1. Overreliance on Ads:

- *User Experience:* Excessive ads can harm the user experience, leading to high bounce rates.

- *Ad Blockers:* With the prevalence of ad blockers, relying solely on ad revenue may limit your income potential.

2. Ignoring Audience Engagement:

- *Quality over Quantity:* Prioritize quality content and engagement over a high volume of mediocre posts.

- *Neglecting Comments:* Ignoring comments and social media interactions can alienate your audience.

3. Inauthentic Promotion:

- *Trust Issues:* Promoting products solely for profit without genuine belief can erode trust with your audience.

- *Product Relevance:* Ensure promoted products align with your blog's theme and provide value to your audience.

4. Ignoring SEO Best Practices:

- *Failure to Adapt:* Neglecting SEO updates and best practices can result in a decline in search engine rankings.

- *Keyword Stuffing:* Overusing keywords can harm your content's readability and credibility.

5. Inconsistent Posting Schedule:

- *Loss of Interest:* Irregular posting can lead to a loss of audience interest and decreased traffic.

- *SEO Impact:* Consistency is crucial for maintaining and improving search engine rankings.

6. Neglecting Mobile Optimization:

- *Mobile Traffic:* With a significant portion of internet users accessing content on mobile devices, neglecting mobile optimization can lead to a loss of traffic.

- *Google Rankings:* Mobile-friendliness is a factor in Google's ranking algorithm.

7. Not Adapting to Trends:

- *Stagnation:* Failing to adapt to emerging trends can result in stagnation and reduced relevance.

- *Diversification:* Diversify your content and strategies to stay relevant in a dynamic online landscape.

8. Ignoring Analytics:

- *Lack of Insight:* Neglecting analytics tools hinders your ability to understand audience behavior, preferences, and content performance.

- *Missed Opportunities:* Analytics provide insights for optimizing content, refining strategies, and identifying monetization opportunities.

In conclusion, blogging for profit requires a strategic approach, continuous adaptation, and a commitment to building authentic relationships with your audience. By implementing effective strategies and avoiding common pitfalls, bloggers can navigate the evolving landscape of content creation and turn their passion into a sustainable and profitable venture.

- Podcasting and Online Video: Turning Content into Cash

In the ever-evolving landscape of digital content, podcasting and online video have emerged as powerful mediums not only for creative expression but also as lucrative avenues for turning content into cash. This discussion explores the strategies and opportunities within the realms of podcasting and online video, shedding light on how creators can effectively monetize their content while navigating the challenges of these dynamic platforms.

Podcasting Strategies:

1. Audience Engagement:

- Build a Dedicated Audience: Cultivate a loyal listener base through engaging content, consistent scheduling, and active audience interaction.

- Utilize Calls to Action (CTAs): Encourage audience participation, reviews, and subscriptions to enhance visibility.

2. Monetization Models:

- Sponsorships and Advertisements: Partner with brands for sponsored content or integrate ads into your podcast episodes.

- Listener Support: Utilize platforms like Patreon or listener support programs to receive financial contributions from your audience.

- Affiliate Marketing: Promote relevant products or services and earn a commission for every sale through your affiliate links.

3. Exclusive Content and Memberships:

- *Patreon or Memberships:* Offer premium, exclusive content to subscribers willing to support your podcast through membership platforms.

- *Bonus Episodes or Series:* Create additional content for paying subscribers to enhance the value proposition.

4. Live Events and Merchandising:

- *Live Shows:* Organize live podcast events or virtual gatherings for your audience, charging admission or receiving donations.

- *Merchandising:* Design and sell merchandise related to your podcast, such as branded apparel or accessories.

5. Collaborations and Partnerships:

- *Guest Appearances:* Collaborate with other podcasters, cross-promoting each other's content to expand your reach.

- *Joint Ventures:* Partner with brands or other content creators for mutually beneficial collaborations.

Podcasting Pitfalls:

1. Overlooking Production Quality:

- *Audio Quality:* Poor audio quality can drive away listeners. Invest in decent recording equipment and editing software.

- *Inconsistent Release Schedule:* Maintain a consistent release schedule to keep your audience engaged.

2. Ignoring Audience Feedback:

- *Interactive Approach:* Engage with your audience through social media, emails, or live sessions. Ignoring feedback can lead to disengagement.

- *Failure to Adapt:* Be open to adapting your content based on audience preferences and changing trends.

3. Overemphasis on Monetization:

- *Balancing Act:* While monetization is essential, a relentless focus on profit may compromise content quality and authenticity.

- *Alienating the Audience:* Too many ads or constant requests for support can turn listeners away.

Online Video Strategies:

1. YouTube Monetization:

- *Ad Revenue:* Join the YouTube Partner Program to earn revenue through ads displayed on your videos.

- *Channel Memberships:* Offer channel memberships for exclusive perks and content for paying subscribers.

2. Brand Partnerships and Sponsored Content:

- *Collaborate with Brands:* Partner with brands for sponsored content, product placements, or brand integrations.

- Affiliate Marketing: Incorporate affiliate links in video descriptions to earn commissions for products or services promoted.

3. Crowdfunding and Fan Support:

- Patreon or Ko-fi: Invite your audience to support your content through crowdfunding platforms in exchange for exclusive perks.

- Donation Platforms: Encourage direct donations or tips during live streams or through platforms like Buy Me a Coffee.

4. Online Courses and Workshops:

- Educational Content: Create and sell online courses or workshops related to your niche.

- Webinars and Virtual Classes: Host live sessions for a fee, providing valuable insights or skills to your audience.

5. Merchandising and E-commerce:

- Branded Merchandise: Design and sell merchandise related to your online video content.

- Digital Products: Offer digital products like eBooks, presets, or digital artwork for purchase.

Online Video Pitfalls:

1. **Ignoring SEO and Discoverability:**

- Optimized Titles and Descriptions: Neglecting SEO practices can hinder video discoverability. Use relevant titles, descriptions, and tags.

- Consistency and Quality: Inconsistent content quality or upload frequency can impact your video's ranking on search and recommendation algorithms.

2. **Failing to Engage Viewers:**

- Call to Action (CTA): Encourage viewers to like, share, subscribe, and leave comments. Engaging content keeps viewers interested.

- Neglecting Analytics: Regularly analyze viewer demographics, watch time, and engagement metrics to refine your content strategy.

3. Lack of Diversification:

- *Platform Dependence:* Relying solely on one platform can be risky. Explore multiple platforms to diversify your audience and income streams.

- *Adaptability:* Platforms evolve; be prepared to adapt to changes in algorithms, policies, or emerging platforms.

Successfully turning content into cash through podcasting and online video requires a strategic approach, dedication, and a keen understanding of your audience. While potential pitfalls exist, they can be navigated with a commitment to authenticity, consistent quality, and a responsive approach to audience feedback. By implementing these strategies and avoiding common pitfalls, content creators can turn their passion into a sustainable and profitable venture in the competitive landscape of podcasting and online video.

- Leveraging Social Media for Monetization

Social media platforms have evolved beyond mere communication tools, transforming into powerful ecosystems for content creation, community building, and, importantly, monetization. This discussion explores strategies and considerations for creators aiming to turn their social media presence into a sustainable source of income.

1. **Building a Strong Personal Brand:**

   - *Consistent Branding:* Maintain a cohesive brand identity across all platforms, including a recognizable profile picture, consistent username, and cohesive visuals.

   - *Authenticity:* Showcase your personality and values to build an authentic connection with your audience.

2. Choosing the Right Platforms:

- *Audience Analysis:* Understand your target audience and identify the platforms where they are most active.

- *Diversification:* Utilize multiple platforms to reach a broader audience but focus on the ones most aligned with your content and goals.

3. Content Monetization Models:

- *Ad Revenue:* Some platforms offer ad revenue-sharing programs based on views and engagement (e.g., YouTube AdSense).

- *Affiliate Marketing:* Promote products or services and earn a commission for each sale through affiliate links.

- *Sponsored Content:* Partner with brands for sponsored posts, collaborations, or product placements.

- *Digital Products:* Sell digital products like eBooks, presets, or online courses directly to your audience.

- *Membership and Subscriptions:* Offer exclusive content or perks to paying subscribers.

4. Engagement and Community Building:

- *Interactivity:* Encourage audience participation through polls, Q&A sessions, and live videos.

- *Community Platforms:* Consider creating a private community or utilizing platform-specific features like Facebook Groups or Patreon for more intimate interactions.

5. Optimizing for SEO and Discoverability:

- *Effective Use of Hashtags:* Research and use relevant hashtags to improve the discoverability of your content.

- *Keywords and Descriptions:* Incorporate keywords in your profile bio and content descriptions to enhance search ability.

6. Partnerships and Collaborations:

- *Cross-Promotions:* Collaborate with other creators for cross-promotions, expanding your reach to each other's audiences.

- *Brand Collaborations:* Partner with brands that align with your values and resonate with your audience.

7. Utilizing Paid Features and Tools:

- *Promoted Posts and Ads:* Invest in sponsored content or ads to increase visibility and reach a wider audience.

- *Platform Features:* Explore premium features on platforms like Instagram or Twitter for additional visibility and engagement.

8. Consistent Posting Schedule:

- *Algorithmic Favorability:* Consistent posting helps algorithms favor your content, increasing its visibility in users' feeds.

- Audience Expectations: Establish a posting schedule that aligns with your audience's expectations and engagement patterns.

9. Diversification of Income Streams:

- Avoiding Dependence: Relying on a single income stream is risky. Diversify by incorporating multiple monetization methods.

- Adaptability: Be open to exploring new income streams and adapting to changes in the social media landscape.

10. Data Analytics and Performance Tracking:

- Platform Analytics: Regularly analyze platform-specific analytics to understand audience behavior, demographics, and engagement metrics.

- Refinement and Optimization: Use data insights to refine your content strategy, posting times, and monetization approaches.

Considerations and Potential Pitfalls:

1. **Platform Policies and Changes:**

- *Stay Informed:* Keep abreast of changes in algorithms, policies, and features on each platform.

- *Adaptability:* Be prepared to adapt your strategies as platforms evolve.

2. **Balancing Monetization and Content Quality:**

- *Value Proposition:* Prioritize delivering value to your audience over aggressive monetization.

- *Authenticity:* Ensure that sponsored content aligns with your brand and does not compromise authenticity.

3. **Audience Trust and Relationships:**

- *Transparent Communication:* Be transparent with your audience about sponsored content and affiliate partnerships.

- *Building Trust:* Prioritize building trust with your audience by delivering on promises and maintaining authenticity.

4. Platform Dependency:

- *Diversification:* Avoid relying solely on one platform. Diversify your presence to mitigate risks associated with algorithm changes or account issues.

5. Burnout and Consistency:

- *Realistic Scheduling:* Set realistic posting schedules to avoid burnout while maintaining consistency.

- *Quality Over Quantity:* Prioritize quality content over excessive posting.

6. Legal and Ethical Considerations:

- *Disclosure:* disclose paid partnerships and affiliate relationships to comply with legal and ethical standards.

- *Privacy Concerns:* Be mindful of privacy concerns, both yours and your audience's, when utilizing certain features or collecting data.

Leveraging social media for monetization is a

dynamic process that requires a strategic blend of creativity, authenticity, and adaptability. Creators who approach monetization with a focus on providing value, building strong connections with their audience, and staying abreast of industry trends are better positioned to thrive in the ever-evolving landscape of social media content creation.

CHAPTER 5:

ACHIEVING TRUE

FINANCIAL FREEDOM

Welcome to the enlightening journey of "Achieving True Financial Freedom." This chapter is your guide to navigating the intricate landscape of personal finance, wealth building, and strategic decision-making that culminates in a life of genuine financial independence. In a world often defined by economic complexities, this exploration is designed to empower you with the knowledge, skills, and mindset needed to break free from financial constraints and embark on a path toward lasting prosperity.

True financial freedom transcends the mere accumulation of wealth; it is a holistic and deliberate approach to managing resources, making informed choices, and aligning your financial goals with your values. In these pages, we will unravel the layers of financial empowerment, from understanding the fundamentals of budgeting and investing to exploring advanced strategies that can elevate your financial standing.

Our journey will delve into the pillars of financial stability, addressing concepts such as debt management, diversified income streams, and building a resilient financial portfolio. Beyond the technical aspects, we'll explore the psychological and behavioral elements that play a pivotal role in achieving and sustaining true financial freedom.

Whether you are starting on the path to financial independence or seeking to refine your existing strategies, this chapter is crafted to provide actionable insights, practical tips, and a comprehensive roadmap to guide you toward your financial aspirations. As we embark on this transformative exploration, remember that achieving true financial freedom is not a destination but a dynamic and continuous process. Embrace the principles laid out here, adapt them to your unique circumstances, and empower yourself to take charge of your financial destiny. Let the journey toward true financial freedom begin.

- Cultivating an Entrepreneurial Mindset

Cultivating an entrepreneurial mindset is a transformative process that goes beyond starting a business; it's about adopting a particular way of thinking and approaching challenges with creativity, resilience, and a proactive attitude. Whether you're an aspiring entrepreneur or aiming to infuse entrepreneurial thinking into your career, the following process can guide you in cultivating an entrepreneurial mindset:

1. **Embrace a Growth Mindset:**

 - *Openness to Learning:* View challenges as opportunities to learn and grow. Embrace a mindset that sees setbacks as stepping stones toward improvement.

- Belief in Development: Understand that abilities and intelligence can be developed through dedication, hard work, and continuous learning.

2. Develop a Vision:

- Long-Term Perspective: Cultivate a clear vision of your goals and aspirations. Understand where you want to go and what impact you want to make.

- Adaptability: Be flexible in adjusting your vision based on evolving circumstances and opportunities.

3. Embrace Risk-Taking:

- Calculated Risks: Learn to assess and take calculated risks. Understand that failure is a part of the entrepreneurial journey and a valuable source of learning.

- Resilience: Develop resilience to bounce back from setbacks, adapting and iterating your approach based on the lessons learned.

4. Innovate and Problem-Solve:

- *Creative Thinking:* Foster a mindset that seeks innovative solutions to problems. Encourage thinking outside the box and exploring unconventional approaches.

- *Problem Identification:* Train yourself to identify problems as opportunities for innovation. Entrepreneurs often thrive by providing solutions to challenges.

5. Build a Network and Collaborate:

- *Relationship Building:* Cultivate a network of like-minded individuals, mentors, and collaborators. Entrepreneurship is often a collective effort.

- *Open to Collaboration:* Be open to collaboration and value the diversity of thought that comes from working with others.

6. Customer-Centric Focus:

- **Understanding Needs:** Develop an understanding of customer needs and preferences.

Entrepreneurs succeed by offering solutions that resonate with their target audience.

 - *Continuous Feedback:* Seek and value feedback from customers, adapting your products or services based on their evolving needs.

 7. **Develop Strong Communication Skills:**

 - *Effective Communication:* Hone your ability to communicate ideas clearly and persuasively. Entrepreneurs often need to articulate their vision to investors, team members, and customers.

 - *Active Listening:* Cultivate active listening skills to understand the needs and concerns of others in your entrepreneurial ecosystem.

 8. **Time Management and Prioritization:**

 - *Prioritize Effectively:* Develop the skill of prioritizing tasks based on their impact and importance. Time management is crucial for handling the multifaceted nature of entrepreneurship.

- *Adaptability:* Be adaptable in adjusting your priorities based on changing circumstances and opportunities.

9. Financial Literacy:

- *Understanding Finances:* Cultivate a solid understanding of financial principles, including budgeting, investment, and risk management.

- *Resource Optimization:* Entrepreneurs make strategic decisions about resource allocation, and financial literacy is crucial for optimizing these decisions.

10. Celebrate Successes and Learn from Failures:

- *Acknowledge Achievements:* Celebrate both small and significant successes along your entrepreneurial journey. Recognize and appreciate your achievements.

- *Reflect on Failures:* When faced with failures, view them as opportunities to learn and improve.

Reflect on the lessons learned and adjust your approach accordingly.

11. Continuous Learning and Adaptation:

- *Curiosity:* Cultivate a curious mindset that seeks to understand industry trends, market dynamics, and emerging technologies.

- *Adapt to Change:* Entrepreneurial environments are dynamic. Develop the ability to adapt to changes in the market, technology, and business landscape.

12. Maintain a Positive Attitude:

- *Optimism:* Nurture an optimistic attitude. A positive mindset can enhance creativity, resilience, and the ability to overcome challenges.

- *Focus on Solutions:* Instead of dwelling on problems, focus on finding solutions and taking proactive steps to address challenges.

Cultivating an entrepreneurial mindset is an ongoing and iterative process. It involves continuous self-reflection, learning from experiences, and adapting to the evolving entrepreneurial landscape. By embracing a growth mindset, being open to new opportunities, and developing the skills and attitudes outlined above, you can foster an entrepreneurial mindset that will not only serve you in business but also in navigating the complexities of life with creativity and resilience.

- Balancing Work and Lifestyle Goals

Balancing work and lifestyle goals is a dynamic and often challenging process that requires planning, self-awareness, and adaptability. Striking the right equilibrium between professional responsibilities and personal fulfilment is crucial for overall well-being and long-term success. Here's a comprehensive guide on the process of balancing work and lifestyle goals:

1. Define Your Values and Priorities:

   - *Reflect on Values:* Clarify your core values and what matters most to you in both your work and personal life.

   - *Prioritize Goals:* Identify and prioritize your short-term and long-term goals in both areas.

2. Set Clear and Realistic Goals:

   - *SMART Goals:* Establish Specific, Measurable, Achievable, Relevant, and Time-bound goals for your work and lifestyle.

   - *Balance Consideration:* Ensure that your goals in both areas align with your overarching vision for a balanced life.

3. **Create a Realistic Schedule:**

   - *Time Blocking:* Allocate specific time blocks for work-related tasks, personal activities, and downtime.

- Flexibility: Allow for flexibility in your schedule to accommodate unexpected events and personal needs.

4. Establish Boundaries:

- Work-Life Boundaries: Clearly define boundaries between work and personal time. Avoid overcommitting to work tasks during personal hours.

- Communication: Communicate your boundaries to colleagues, clients, and family to manage expectations.

5. Prioritize Self-Care:

- Physical Health: Prioritize regular exercise, healthy eating, and sufficient sleep.

- Mental Health: Incorporate practices such as mindfulness, meditation, or hobbies to support mental well-being.

6. Effective Time Management:

- *Prioritization:* Identify and prioritize tasks based on urgency and importance.

- *Eliminate Time Wasters:* Minimize activities that do not contribute significantly to your goals.

7. Delegate and Outsource:

- *Delegate Tasks:* Delegate work tasks that can be handled by others, allowing you to focus on high-priority responsibilities.

- *Outsource Personal Tasks:* Consider outsourcing personal tasks or seeking assistance when needed.

8. Learn to Say No:

- *Setting Boundaries:* Politely decline additional work or personal commitments that may compromise your balance.

- *Effective Communication:* communicate your capacity and commitments to others.

9. **Regularly Evaluate and Adjust:**

- *Periodic Reflection:* Schedule regular check-ins to reflect on your work-life balance and assess whether your goals and priorities have shifted.

- *Adjustments:* Be open to adjusting your approach based on changing circumstances or personal growth.

10. **Invest in Relationships:**

- *Quality Time:* Prioritize quality time with family, friends, and loved ones.

- *Communication:* Maintain open communication with those close to you about your work commitments and ensure their understanding and support.

11. **Celebrate Achievements:**

- *Acknowledge Successes:* Celebrate milestones and achievements in both your work and personal life.

- Gratitude Practice: Cultivate a gratitude practice to appreciate the positive aspects of both spheres.

12. Seek Work-Life Integration:

- Blurring Boundaries Positively: Look for ways to integrate work and personal aspects positively, such as combining a work trip with a personal vacation.

- Holistic Approach: Embrace a holistic approach where each area complements and enhances the other.

13. Continuous Learning and Adaptation:

- Feedback Loop: Solicit feedback from yourself, peers, or mentors to gauge your work-life balance effectiveness.

- Adaptability: Be adaptable and willing to make changes based on insights gained from experience.

14. **Financial Planning:**

- *Financial Goals:* Set financial goals that align with your desired lifestyle, including savings, investments, and budgeting.

- *Long-Term Planning:* Consider long-term financial planning to support future lifestyle aspirations.

15. **Model Healthy Work-Life Integration:**

- *Leadership Example:* If in a leadership role, model healthy work-life integration for your team.

- *Encourage Balance:* Promote a workplace culture that values and supports work-life balance.

16. **Seek Professional Support:**

- *Career Coaching:* Consider seeking the guidance of a career coach to align your career path with lifestyle goals.

- *Therapeutic Support:* If needed, seek professional therapeutic support to manage stress, anxiety, or challenges.

Balancing work and lifestyle goals is an ongoing process that evolves with changing circumstances and priorities. By implementing these strategies and maintaining a proactive approach, you can cultivate a harmonious integration of work and personal life, fostering not only professional success but also overall well-being and fulfilment. Remember, achieving balance is a continuous journey, and adapting to new circumstances is a key element in maintaining equilibrium.

- Scaling Your Online Business for Long-Term Success

Scaling an online business for long-term success involves strategic planning, efficient execution, and continuous adaptation to evolving market trends. Here's a comprehensive guide to the process of scaling your online business:

1. **Evaluate Current Operations:**

 - *Performance Analysis:* Conduct a thorough analysis of your current business operations, identifying strengths, weaknesses, opportunities, and threats.

 - *Customer Feedback:* Gather feedback from customers to understand their needs and expectations.

2. **Set Clear Goals and Objectives:**

 - *Quantifiable Targets:* Establish clear and measurable goals for your business, such as revenue targets, customer acquisition goals, and market expansion.

 - *Long-Term Vision:* Align your short-term objectives with a long-term vision for sustainable growth.

3. **Optimize Your Online Presence:**

 - *Website and UX:* Ensure your website is user-friendly, mobile-responsive, and optimized for search engines.

- Social Media Strategy: Leverage social media platforms to enhance your brand presence and engage with your audience.

4. Invest in Marketing and Advertising:

- Digital Marketing: Allocate resources to effective digital marketing strategies, including SEO, content marketing, and paid advertising.

- Social Media Advertising: Utilize targeted social media advertising to reach specific audience segments.

5. *Expand Product or Service Offerings:*

- Diversification: Introduce new products or services that complement your existing offerings.

- Market Research: Conduct market research to identify gaps or trends that align with your business niche.

6. Optimize Supply Chain and Logistics:

- Efficient Processes: Streamline your supply chain and logistics processes to improve efficiency and reduce costs.

- Inventory Management: Implement effective inventory management systems to prevent stock outs and overstock situations.

7. **Automate Repetitive Tasks:**

- Workflow Automation: Identify tasks that can be automated to improve efficiency and reduce manual workload.

- Technology Integration: Implement tools and software that streamline processes, such as customer relationship management (CRM) systems and e-commerce platforms.

8. **Enhance Customer Experience:**

- Personalization: Implement personalized customer experiences through tailored recommendations and communication.

- Customer Support: Invest in responsive customer support to address inquiries, concerns, and feedback.

9. Build a Scalable Team:

- Talent Acquisition: Recruit skilled professionals who align with your business goals.

- Training and Development: Invest in continuous training to upskill your team and adapt to industry changes.

10. Explore New Markets:

- Geographic Expansion: Identify opportunities for expanding your business into new geographic markets.

- Internationalization: Consider international markets and adapt your strategy to meet diverse cultural and regulatory considerations.

11. Strategic Partnerships and Collaborations:

- *Industry Alliances:* Forge strategic partnerships with other businesses in your industry to leverage mutual strengths.

- *Affiliate Marketing:* Explore affiliate marketing programs to extend your reach through partner collaborations.

12. **Monitor and Analyze Key Metrics:**

- *Key Performance Indicators (KPIs):* Track and analyze relevant KPIs, such as conversion rates, customer acquisition costs, and customer lifetime value.

- *Data-Driven Decisions:* Make informed decisions based on data insights to refine strategies and operations.

13. **Financial Planning and Investment:**

- *Budget Allocation:* Allocate budget resources effectively to support scaling initiatives.

- *Seek Funding if Necessary:* Consider external funding options if needed to fuel expansion plans.

14. Risk Management:

- *Contingency Planning:* Develop contingency plans to address potential risks and challenges.

- *Adaptability:* Foster a culture of adaptability to navigate unforeseen circumstances.

15. Customer Retention Strategies:

- *Loyalty Programs:* Implement customer loyalty programs to retain existing customers.

- *Feedback Loops:* Encourage customer feedback to identify areas for improvement and innovation.

16. Compliance and Legal Considerations:

- *Stay Informed:* Stay informed about relevant laws and regulations in the regions where you operate.

- *Legal Compliance:* Ensure your business practices adhere to legal standards and industry regulations.

17. Continuous Innovation:

- Research and Development: Invest in research and development to stay ahead of industry trends.

- Adopt Emerging Technologies: Embrace new technologies that can enhance your products, services, or operations.

18. **Measure Sustainable Practices:**

- Environmental Impact: Consider sustainable business practices to align with growing consumer preferences.

- Corporate Social Responsibility: Engage in socially responsible initiatives to build a positive brand image.

19. Community Engagement:

- Brand Building: Engage with your community through social responsibility initiatives and transparent communication.

- Brand Advocacy: Encourage customer advocacy and word-of-mouth marketing.

20. **Regularly Review and Adjust Strategies:**

- Performance Reviews: Regularly review the performance of your scaling strategies against established goals.

- Adaptability: Be willing to adjust strategies based on market feedback, industry trends, and the evolving needs of your business.

Scaling your online business for long-term success is a multifaceted process that requires a holistic approach. By combining strategic planning, leveraging technology, fostering a customer-centric approach, and maintaining adaptability, you can position your business for sustained growth and competitiveness in the dynamic online marketplace. Keep a keen eye on industry trends, customer feedback, and emerging opportunities to stay ahead of the curve as you scale your online business.

CONCLUSION

As we conclude this journey through "How to Make Money Online: The Ultimate Guide to Financial Freedom," I hope the insights shared within these pages have ignited your entrepreneurial spirit and equipped you with the tools to navigate the vast landscape of online opportunities. The pursuit of financial freedom is not merely a destination but a transformative journey, and your commitment to learning, adapting, and taking calculated risks is the compass that will guide you.

In our exploration, we've navigated the digital landscape, delving into the evolution of work, emerging trends, and the foundational steps to building your online presence. We've discussed diverse avenues for online income, from e-commerce to affiliate marketing, freelancing, and the creation of digital products. The chapters on cultivating an entrepreneurial mindset and achieving true financial freedom aimed to empower you not just financially but holistically.

Remember, success is not a one-size-fits-all concept. It's about aligning your financial goals with your unique values and aspirations. The strategies outlined here are your toolkits, but how you wield them is a reflection of your creativity, determination, and resilience.

As you embark on your journey, embrace the challenges as opportunities and view setbacks as stepping stones to growth. Stay curious, stay hungry for knowledge, and, above all, stay true to your vision. Financial freedom is not about amassing wealth for its own sake but about gaining the freedom to live life on your terms, pursuing your passions, and making a positive impact.

In the ever-evolving landscape of the online world, flexibility and adaptability are your greatest allies. Embrace change, stay attuned to market dynamics, and be open to refining your strategies. Remember that mistakes are not failures but invaluable lessons that propel you forward.

I want to express my sincere gratitude for joining me in this exploration. Your commitment to self-improvement and financial empowerment is a testament to your potential for success. As you step into the dynamic realm of online entrepreneurship, may you find fulfilment, purpose, and the financial freedom you aspire to.

This is not a farewell but an invitation to view this conclusion as a new beginning. The journey toward financial freedom is ongoing, and your story is still unfolding. May your path be filled with prosperity, meaningful connections, and the satisfaction of knowing that you have the knowledge and tools to shape your financial destiny?

Here's to your success, your growth, and your unwavering pursuit of financial freedom. The future is yours to create, and I have full confidence that it holds incredible opportunities for you.